America: Land of the Fee?

Feeconomics & Ferengi Commerce In The USA

Gary Gansson

Dedicated To
Tran Nguyen

Introduction

In the land of opportunity and innovation, where dreams are pursued and ambitions kindled, another facet of the American experience has quietly entrenched itself within the very fabric of society. As we step into the intricate world of financial dealings and economic complexities, it becomes evident that the concept of "America: Land of the Fee" holds more truth than meets the eye. Just as the Ferengi species from the distant reaches of the Star Trek universe embody a commerce-based culture of thinking and living, modern America finds itself navigating a landscape dominated by fees and charges. This book embarks on a journey through the labyrinthine landscapes of these fees, charges, and costs that have become an inseparable part of modern American life.

Mapping the Fee Terrain

To truly understand the contemporary state of fees in America, we must trace its roots back through history. From the early days of frontier trading posts to the rise of industrialization, the concept of paying for services, conveniences, and access has evolved in tandem with the nation itself. Much like the Ferengi, whose economic pursuits define their way of life, the notion of fees in America is deeply interwoven with the entrepreneurial spirit that has driven the country's economic growth. This prompts us to question whether this quest for innovation has unintentionally paved the way for a fee-centered economy, akin to the Ferengi's relentless pursuit of profit.

A Fee for Every Occasion

Venturing into the bustling streets of any American city or town, one cannot escape the reality that fees have seamlessly integrated into every facet of daily life. From the moment we wake, the digital alarm clock's electricity silently accrues its fee, setting the stage for the financial interactions that await us. As we move through the day, we encounter an array of fees: the convenience fee for our morning coffee, the service fee for a ride-share to work, the subscription fee for streaming entertainment, and even the ATM fee for accessing our hard-earned money. These seemingly innocuous charges, while individually modest, collectively amount to a significant portion of our earnings.

The Layers of Financial Realities

To navigate the intricate landscape of fees, we must also understand the layers of financial realities that individuals face. Just as the Ferengi culture revolves around complex negotiations and economic strategies, from the urban professional to the rural farmer, from the college student to the retiree, each demographic grapples with fees in unique ways. The impact of fees extends beyond mere financial transactions; it influences decisions, behaviors, and aspirations. In the pursuit of upward mobility and financial security, individuals often find themselves caught between the promise of convenience and the weight of extra costs.

This book aims to shed light on these multifaceted dimensions of fees, much like the way scholars analyze the intricacies of the Ferengi's economic system. It is a comprehensive exploration of a phenomenon that impacts us all—whether we're swiping our credit cards at the grocery store, deciphering the breakdown of our cellphone bills, or contemplating the true cost of our educational aspirations. We delve into the systems that propagate fees, the industries that profit from them, and the individuals who grapple with their implications.

Amidst the complexity, a glimmer of hope emerges. This book is not just a dissection of fees; it is an attempt to make sense of this fee economy. By understanding the history, psychology, and mechanics of fees, we equip ourselves with the knowledge to make informed decisions, advocate for transparency, and envision a future where financial empowerment prevails. As we embark on this journey through the intricate tapestry of fees in America, let us unravel the threads that bind us to the "Land of the Fee," seeking to transform it into a realm of informed choices, equitable practices, and shared prosperity.

Chapter 1: The Fee Economy

In the annals of American economic history, an evolution has occurred that parallels the intriguing cultural phenomenon observed in the Ferengi species of the Star Trek universe. Much like the Ferengi, whose very way of life revolves around commerce, the modern American economy has witnessed the meteoric rise of fees, entwining them so intricately that they have become a defining characteristic of financial transactions. As we delve into this chapter, we peel back the layers of the fee economy, drawing parallels between the Ferengi's commerce-based culture and America's evolving relationship with fees.

From Anomalies to Norms

In the realm of commerce, fees were once anomalies—occasional and modest charges tacked onto services and transactions. However, the landscape has shifted, and much like the Ferengi's gradual progression from modest traders to shrewd negotiators, fees have transitioned from occasional expenses to integral components of daily life. With each swipe of a card, each online transaction, or each service availed, fees now accompany us, oftentimes unnoticed until they collectively shape our financial realities.

Drawing inspiration from the Ferengi's knack for converting every interaction into a potential profit, American businesses have ingeniously devised various types of fees that cater to almost every conceivable transaction. The fee ecosystem has become an ever-expanding galaxy of charges: convenience fees, processing fees, subscription fees, service fees—the list is as extensive as the Ferengi Rules of Acquisition (see the appendix).

The Subtle Economics of Fees

The Ferengi culture, heavily steeped in trade and barter, values the acquisition of wealth above all else. Similarly, the economic landscape of modern America is marked by its own set of motivations that have driven the proliferation of fees. This section delves into the economic factors contributing to the prevalence of fees, akin to the Ferengi's unwavering pursuit of profit.

As the financial world advances, the symbiotic relationship between businesses seeking growth and consumers seeking convenience has given rise to an environment where fees are positioned as the cost of access to products and services. Just as the Ferengi see opportunity in every interaction, businesses see potential revenue streams in each service they offer. This transformation from occasional fees to fee-centric models is not coincidental; it's a calculated strategy influenced by supply and demand, innovation, and the competitive market.

The Fee-Based Society

Much like the Ferengi prioritize profit as a cornerstone of their society, fees have become an integral part of the American economic and social fabric. In a culture that values efficiency, speed, and convenience, fees are often accepted as a necessary compromise. While the Ferengi may perceive profit as an indicator of success, American society is navigating the complexities of viewing fees as a trade-off for convenience.

The intersection of technology and business has given rise to a society that functions on the swift exchange of goods and services, often accompanied by a fee. Just as the Ferengi prioritize negotiations, the modern American consumer is often faced with negotiating the terms of fees—seeking discounts, avoiding surcharges, or comparing options to minimize the impact on their financial well-being.

Through the lens of the Ferengi's relentless pursuit of commerce, this chapter highlights the evolution of fees into a cornerstone of the American economy. Just as the Ferengi have perfected the art of trade, American businesses have refined the practice of fee-based transactions. As we journey through this chapter, it becomes evident that the intersection of the Ferengi's commerce-based culture and America's fee economy share more than mere parallels—they provide insight into the intricate workings of a society where transactions are no longer just exchanges, but rather strategic interactions with financial implications.

Chapter 2: The Cost of Convenience

In a universe not so distant, the Ferengi of Star Trek fame boldly embody a culture where commerce reigns supreme. As we step into the realm of convenience services, it's tempting to imagine the Ferengi rubbing their lobes in anticipation, for the fee-based landscape mirrors their relentless pursuit of profit. However, even for these masters of trade, the allure of convenience comes at a price, and here on Earth, in the Land of the Fee, we're about to explore the fascinating dynamics of convenience, fees, and the complex psychology of modern consumerism.

The Convenience Fee Universe

In a world where online shopping, food delivery, and ride-sharing are at our fingertips, the Ferengi's maxim "Profit is its own reward" finds resonance in the realm of convenience services. In the age of the Ferengi, such services would likely be part of the daily hustle, with convenience fees meticulously calculated to maximize profit. On Earth, this is not far from reality. As we examine the convenience fees that accompany these services, we find ourselves caught in a paradox: paying to simplify our lives, yet contributing to the coffers of businesses aiming to simplify their bottom line.

Much like the Ferengi's tendency to capitalize on opportunities, businesses have seized upon the human desire for convenience and created a fee structure that monetizes it. The convenience fee dances along the edge of reason and reality, much like a Ferengi dance of joy at a particularly profitable transaction.

The Psyche of Convenience

The Ferengi have a saying: "Greed is eternal." In our own consumer-driven society, this sentiment finds its counterpart in the psychology of convenience. The willingness to pay a premium for convenience can be attributed to a blend of time scarcity, comfort, and the instant gratification that mirrors the Ferengi's desire for immediate profit. Just as the Ferengi equate profit with success, modern consumers equate convenience with quality of life.

Delving into this psychological terrain, we unearth the trade-offs that accompany the pursuit of convenience. Like the Ferengi's penchant for negotiation, individuals often negotiate with themselves—weighing the added fee against the time saved or the comfort gained. The human psyche dances a delicate tango with the allure of ease, and the fee becomes the tune to which we step.

Convenience vs. Contentment

As the Ferengi say, "Satisfaction is not guaranteed," and the same holds true for our Earthly pursuit of convenience. The question arises: Does the added cost truly enhance our quality of life? Much like a Ferengi's complex negotiations, evaluating convenience fees necessitates a nuanced approach.

Just as Ferengi society places a high value on accumulating wealth, modern society often prioritizes accumulating experiences. But do these experiences, draped in the allure of convenience, truly enrich our lives? As we tread the path paved with convenience fees, we're confronted with the reality that the pursuit of ease can sometimes detract from the very essence of the experience we're seeking to enhance.

In a twist worthy of Ferengi plot twists, we must ponder whether convenience, once so dearly paid for, eventually leads to convenience fatigue—a feeling not unlike the Ferengi realizing that another acquisition does not, in fact, bring lasting satisfaction.

This chapter, much like the Ferengi's intricate schemes, peels back the layers of convenience, exposing the intricacies of the convenience fee universe. As we navigate through these layers, we're challenged to embrace the wisdom of the Ferengi's Rule of Acquisition #76: "Every once in a while, declare peace. It confuses the hell out of your enemies." In our own consumer journeys, declaring peace might involve questioning whether the added cost of convenience truly leads to the harmonious enrichment of our lives or merely confuses our financial equilibrium.

Chapter 3: Navigating the Financial System

In the far reaches of the cosmos, on the Ferengi homeworld of Ferenginar, the majestic Tower of Commerce stands tall, an emblem of a culture where profit reigns supreme. Here on Earth, as we delve into the labyrinthine world of banking fees, one might imagine a parallel in the intricate structure of the Tower of Commerce. But while the Ferengi's pursuit of profit might be admirable in their commerce-centered universe, the realities of banking fees here on Earth warrant a closer look, a touch of humor, and a dose of sobering reality.

Unraveling the Fee Web

Imagine entering the Tower of Commerce on Ferenginar, where every floor is a testament to a different facet of profit. Our own banking system is similarly complex, replete with fees that parallel the Ferengi's zeal for trade. ATM usage fees, overdraft fees, maintenance fees—all woven into the very fabric of our financial lives. It's as if each fee is a floor of the Tower, each transaction a staircase leading us further into the heart of the financial system.

As we analyze these banking fees, we're confronted with the reality that, unlike the Ferengi's open embrace of commerce, we often navigate the financial system unaware of the fees lurking around each corner. The Tower of Commerce may be a towering symbol of Ferengi culture, but the fee-laden corridors of our own banking system are a labyrinth where individuals may find themselves entangled in a web of charges.

Guiding Through the Financial Maze

In the Ferengi culture, negotiation is an art form—a dance that defines their interactions. On Earth, our dance with the financial system demands a different kind of artistry: the art of making informed choices to minimize banking-related fees. Just as the Ferengi carefully strategize their business dealings, individuals must strategize their banking interactions to avoid unnecessary charges.

This section serves as a guide to those navigating the modern banking landscape. It's akin to deciphering the nuanced Ferengi Rules of Acquisition; here, the goal is to decode the fine print of bank agreements, choose fee-friendly accounts, and optimize transaction behavior. By approaching our financial dealings with the wisdom of a seasoned Ferengi negotiator, we can potentially avoid the pitfalls of excessive banking fees.

Fee Impact on the Margins

While the Ferengi society may exude the appearance of financial equality, our own society grapples with disparities that mirror the stratification of the Ferengi castes. For vulnerable and underserved communities, the burden of banking fees weighs heavier—a reality that echoes the experiences of the Ferengi lesser castes. The Tower of Commerce on Ferenginar stands as an aspiration for all, but not all are able to ascend its heights.

This section explores the impact of fees on marginalized communities, highlighting the way banking fees can exacerbate financial inequalities. Much like the social strata within Ferengi society, the disparities in fee burdens on Earth are a stark reminder of the urgent need for equitable financial access. It's a call to action—to examine the ways in which fees, like the layers of the Tower of Commerce, can obscure the view of financial empowerment for those who need it most.

Navigating the financial system isn't unlike exploring the Tower of Commerce—each floor, each fee, each interaction a step toward understanding a complex ecosystem. As we move through this chapter, we're reminded that while the Ferengi thrive in their world of commerce, we must thrive in ours by advocating for transparent banking practices, arming ourselves with knowledge, and working collectively to ensure that our financial systems serve the many, not just the few.

Chapter 4: The Education Dilemma

In the realm of the cosmos, where planets and civilizations weave intricate narratives, the Ferengi species presents an economic tapestry unlike any other. But here on Earth, as we step into the education sector, we encounter a storyline that, while devoid of Ferengi lobes, is equally captivating and complex. The parallels between the education system's fee predicaments and the Ferengi pursuit of profit offer both a source of humor and a sobering reminder of the gravity of the challenges we face.

The Price of Knowledge

Imagine a Ferengi trader haggling for the price of knowledge—it's a concept foreign to their world but familiar to ours. As we peer into the educational landscape, we're greeted by the rising costs of education and a profusion of fees reminiscent of Ferengi bargaining. Application fees, tuition hikes, and textbook costs are the currency of our education system, akin to the Ferengi's obsession with wealth accumulation.

In the Ferengi's pursuit of acquisition, they embrace commerce as the path to success. Similarly, the modern education system, while aiming to empower minds, often comes at the cost of financial strain. It's as if the Ferengi's unquenchable desire for profit manifests in the education system's unquenchable thirst for funds.

Debts and Degrees

In the Ferengi universe, profit is revered above all else. On Earth, a parallel can be drawn to the financial implications of higher education. The concept of student loans—a debt-driven investment in one's future—is akin to the Ferengi's relentless pursuit of profit, albeit with potential long-term consequences.

The education dilemma is illuminated by student loans and the financial burden they pose. Just as the Ferengi's rule "A contract is a contract is a contract" is gospel, so too is the reality that student loans must be repaid. The pursuit of education should ideally be an investment in one's future, much like the Ferengi's pursuit of business ventures. However, the specter of student loan debts introduces a discordant note—an echo of the Ferengi's profit-driven existence, but with a human twist.

Rethinking the Quadrivium

In a universe where the Ferengi epitomize capitalism, our Earthly pursuit of education begs for reform. Imagine if the Ferengi's famed Quadrivium—Acquisition, Lying, Bribery, and Treachery—were replaced with a Quadrivium of Equitable Education: Accessibility, Affordability, Inclusivity, and Quality.

This section delves into alternatives and reforms, each element of the Quadrivium serving as a stepping stone toward a more just and accessible education system. It's a call to action that mirrors the Ferengi's entrepreneurial zeal—only this time, the goal is not mere profit, but a society where knowledge isn't a privilege but a birthright.

Navigating the education dilemma is a quest that parallels the Ferengi's tireless search for profit. As we explore the rising costs, implications of debts, and potential solutions, we're reminded that while the Ferengi's pursuit of acquisition is a cultural norm, our pursuit of equitable education should be an imperative for societal progress. The echoes of the Ferengi's rule "Greed is eternal" should be drowned out by the resounding chorus of voices demanding a world where education transcends fees and becomes a beacon of hope for all.

Chapter 5: Healthcare Costs and Hurdles

In the cosmos of Star Trek, where cultures and species intertwine, the Ferengi stand as a testament to the power of commerce. As we delve into the realm of healthcare costs, it's impossible not to draw parallels between the intricate web of fees that ensnare patients and the Ferengi's artful negotiations. Yet, in our exploration of this chapter, we find ourselves navigating a narrative that marries the Ferengi's acumen with the sobering reality of healthcare access.

The Currency of Wellness

Picture a Ferengi merchant bartering for life-saving medicine—it's a scene seldom witnessed in their universe. However, our Earthly healthcare landscape bears a resemblance, with insurance premiums, co-pays, and prescription costs forming the currency of wellness. Much like the Ferengi's unrelenting drive for profit, our healthcare system's reliance on fees can often overshadow the pursuit of well-being.

In the Ferengi's world, acquisition is a virtue; in ours, healthcare is a right. Yet, the financial hurdles patients face echo the Ferengi's relentless pursuit of wealth. It's as if our society struggles to reconcile the notion of fees with the imperative of health, creating a tension that, like the Ferengi's profit-driven ethos, can overshadow the true purpose of the endeavor.

The Barrier of Bills

The Ferengi's obsession with wealth might not be alien to the financial obstacles individuals face in seeking healthcare. From the Ferengi's point of view, profit is worth any effort—a sentiment mirrored in the exorbitant healthcare fees that often hinder access to services. Just as the Ferengi might engage in ruthless negotiations, patients too engage in a negotiation of a different kind—one where financial well-being meets physical well-being.

The healthcare challenges we face are akin to a Ferengi's elaborate scheme to extract profit. Navigating insurance networks, deciphering medical bills, and strategizing co-payments can feel as complex as the Ferengi's rulebook. The burden of these fees forms a barrier, one that often stands between individuals and the care they need.

Healing the System

The Ferengi's motto "The bigger the smile, the sharper the knife" finds an unlikely parallel in the state of our healthcare system. However, there is room for reform. Just as the Ferengi can learn the value of cooperation beyond profit, so too can we envision a healthcare system that transcends financial barriers.

This section delves into potential solutions, much like the Ferengi might contemplate a new venture. Universal healthcare, fee transparency, and innovative funding models are explored as avenues toward making healthcare affordable and accessible for all. It's a reminder that while the Ferengi value profit, our society values health—a value that should be embraced by a healthcare system designed to heal, not just to profit.

In our quest to unravel the layers of healthcare fees and challenges, we're reminded that just as the Ferengi's quest for wealth has its limits, our healthcare system's quest for financial gain should not override its fundamental purpose. The echoes of the Ferengi's pursuit of acquisition should fade into the background as we work collectively to create a healthcare system that prioritizes health, compassion, and the well-being of all.

Chapter 6: The Real Estate Rollercoaster

In the cosmos where interstellar civilizations converge, the Ferengi species shine as paragons of commerce. Here on Earth, as we step into the world of real estate, the echoes of the Ferengi's famed Rules of Acquisition reverberate through a realm where fees are as intricate and nuanced as the Ferengi's complex transactions. Join us as we venture into this chapter, where real estate parallels Ferengi dealings and financial tales unfold in our very own "Land of the Fee."

The House of Transaction

Imagine a Ferengi trader showcasing a coveted item, ready to strike a deal. In our world, the housing market similarly involves an intricate dance of negotiations, accompanied by a symphony of fees. Realtor commissions, closing costs, and property taxes populate the landscape, each fee an integral note in the melody of a real estate transaction.

Like the Ferengi's Rule of Acquisition #18—"A Ferengi without profit is no Ferengi at all"—our housing market seems to uphold a similar sentiment. The fervor to secure profit is palpable in the real estate fees that seem to materialize at every corner. It's a reminder that, just as the Ferengi's commerce defines their culture, the world of real estate is shaped by a culture where fees are an inextricable part of the pursuit of property.

The Tenant's Gambit

In the realm of Ferengi commerce, strategy and shrewdness reign supreme. On Earth, the same attributes are required of renters navigating a market teeming with fees. The Ferengi's Rule of Acquisition #76, "Every once in a while, declare peace. It confuses the hell out of your enemies," finds its parallel in the tenant's careful negotiation with landlords to minimize fees and secure a home.

For those aspiring to become first-time homebuyers, the parallels are evident. As the Ferengi strive to maximize profits, individuals strive to maximize their investment by minimizing real estate fees. Closing costs and property taxes are the hurdles to be overcome, reminiscent of the Ferengi's knack for calculating costs and profits to achieve the best deal.

Housing Dreams and Innovations

In the Ferengi universe, economic prowess is the key to success. Our own pursuit of housing stability has given rise to creative models aiming to mitigate the impact of fees. As the Ferengi's Rule of Acquisition #10 states, "Greed is eternal," but so is the quest for innovative solutions.

This section explores co-housing, tiny homes, and other innovative housing models that address the challenges posed by real estate fees. Just as the Ferengi value ingenuity in their business endeavors, we too are embracing new strategies to navigate the complexities of the real estate market. It's a reminder that while fees may be a constant, the ways in which we approach them can be ever-evolving.

As we traverse the real estate rollercoaster, where fees rise and fall like Ferengi profit margins, we're reminded that the pursuit of a home transcends mere transactions. The echoes of the Ferengi's commercial endeavors are met with the challenge of balancing the aspiration for property with the quest for equitable access. It's an intricate dance, where innovation meets affordability, and where, much like the Ferengi, we seek to find a balance between the pursuit of profit and the creation of a better future.

Chapter 7: Investing and Retirement

In the expansive universe of Star Trek, where species forge their destinies amidst galaxies of intrigue, the Ferengi stand out as emblematic of commerce's might. As we navigate the world of investments and retirement planning, it's hard not to summon the Ferengi's Rules of Acquisition as guiding stars in a constellation of financial possibilities. In this chapter, we embark on a voyage where investment fees meet retirement dreams, and where echoes of the Ferengi's commerce-based ethos converge with Earthly financial realities.

The Profit Pathway

Imagine a Ferengi speculator considering investments—it's an image that mirrors our own world's approach to financial growth. In the Ferengi's pursuit of profit, every deal is a dance, much like our world's maneuvering through investment products, from mutual funds to ETFs. And just as the Ferengi's Rule of Acquisition #48 states, "The bigger the smile, the sharper the knife," our investments often come with smiles on the surface, but the knife of fees beneath.

Like the Ferengi's trading endeavors, our investments have a layer of complexity—fees that may seem modest, yet can accrue to substantial sums over time. It's as if each investment fee is a reminder of the Ferengi's philosophy that profit is worth every negotiation, even if hidden beneath layers of transactions.

The Time Horizon

In the Ferengi's universe, wealth accumulates over time, driven by the principle that "A deal is a deal... until a better one comes along." Our Earthly investments share this long-term perspective, particularly in the context of retirement planning. Just as the Ferengi envision each transaction as a step toward greater wealth, individuals envision each investment as a step toward a secure retirement.

Yet, much like the Ferengi's trading strategies, investment fees can impact the long-term success of our retirement plans. It's akin to the Ferengi's Rule of Acquisition #98, "Every man has his price." Our investments, too, have a price—a fee that chips away at the potential growth of our retirement savings. The echoes of the Ferengi's quest for profit are intertwined with our quest for financial security, each fee a factor in determining the extent of our eventual retirement wealth.

Crafting a Financial Future

In the Ferengi's world, the art of negotiation reigns supreme. Our own investment journey demands a different kind of negotiation—a dance with fees, a balancing act between risk and reward. Just as the Ferengi's Rule of Acquisition #13 asserts, "Anything worth doing is worth doing for money," our investments are worth our attention, our knowledge, and our vigilance to minimize fees.

This section offers strategies for building a cost-effective investment portfolio, akin to a Ferengi's strategy for a lucrative deal. Fee-conscious investment choices, tax-efficient approaches, and prudent financial advisory selection all play their part in sculpting a financial future that echoes the Ferengi's tenet: "Satisfaction is not guaranteed."

As we navigate the intricate web of investments and retirement planning, where the Ferengi's business prowess finds its reflection, we're reminded that the journey toward financial security is as much a voyage of calculated decisions as it is a dance with fees. The echoes of the Ferengi's commerce-driven philosophy reverberate in our own investment choices, each choice a step toward a future where the pursuit of profit meets the embrace of prosperity in our golden years.

Chapter 8: Legal and Civic Costs

In the cosmic tableau of Star Trek, where civilizations intersect in a tapestry of narratives, the Ferengi shine as a testament to the power of commerce. As we delve into the realm of legal and civic fees, we find parallels between the Ferengi's Rules of Acquisition and the intricate financial intricacies of our legal system. Join us as we navigate through this chapter, where legal fees and civic participation converge, and where the echoes of the Ferengi's commerce-driven culture intersect with the sobering realities of justice and engagement.

The Litigation Marketplace

Imagine a Ferengi merchant making a case before a tribunal—it's a scenario that melds their penchant for negotiation with our own world's legal intricacies. The legal system's court fees, attorney charges, and fines mirror the Ferengi's dedication to trade and profit. As the Ferengi's Rule of Acquisition #57 states, "Good customers are as rare as latinum. Treasure them," our legal system seems to treasure the revenue generated by fees.

In the Ferengi's universe, commerce is king; in our world, justice should be paramount. Yet, the interplay between legal fees and justice mirrors the Ferengi's pursuit of profit, sometimes overshadowing the pursuit of equity. It's as if the Ferengi's philosophy of financial gain meets the complexities of a justice system where access can be influenced by financial capacity.

The Price of Justice

In the Ferengi's world, transactions are accompanied by negotiations, each party seeking their own profit. Our legal system shares a similar dynamic, where fees are the currency of justice. However, unlike the Ferengi's Rule of Acquisition #286, "When Morn leaves, it's all over," justice should never leave.

The consequences of a system where justice can be influenced by financial capacity echo the Ferengi's philosophy that "Greed is eternal." A parallel exists between the Ferengi's pursuit of accumulation and our own pursuit of fair legal representation—a pursuit that often carries the weight of fees that can strain both our financial well-being and our belief in the fairness of the system.

The Civic Tapestry

In the Ferengi's universe, profit governs decisions. In our own society, civic participation should govern decisions, but financial barriers often act as gatekeepers. Just as the Ferengi's Rule of Acquisition #21 declares, "Never place friendship before profit," we often place financial considerations before civic engagement.

This section explores the broader concept of civic participation and the financial barriers that hinder it. Like the Ferengi's deal-making finesse, our civic engagement is often impacted by fees that may dissuade participation, a reality that runs counter to the ideals of democracy. It's a reminder that while the Ferengi's pursuit of profit may define their society, our pursuit of a just and equitable society should not be restricted by financial barriers.

Navigating the legal and civic landscape is a journey where the echoes of the Ferengi's profit-driven ethos meet the reality of justice and participation. Just as the Ferengi's Rule of Acquisition #98 states, "Every man has his price," we must remember that justice and participation should not be commodities—exchanged for a fee—but rather cornerstones of a society where the pursuit of equity trumps the pursuit of profit.

Chapter 9: Breaking Free from the Fee Cycle

In the boundless expanse of the Star Trek universe, where civilizations intersect and diverge, the Ferengi species stands as a beacon of commerce. As we journey through the final chapter of this book, we find ourselves at the precipice of a profound truth—the interplay of fees and financial realities mirrors the Ferengi's commerce-driven culture. Yet, just as the Ferengi's Rules of Acquisition are not insurmountable, so too can we transcend the labyrinth of fees that shape our own "Land of the Fee." This chapter is a manifesto of empowerment, a declaration that we are not mere participants in a fee economy, but architects of a financial future where equity prevails.

Deciphering the Fee Code

Imagine a Ferengi deciphering a complex contract—it's a scene that mirrors our own quest to decipher the layers of fees we encounter. Just as the Ferengi's Rules of Acquisition guide their trade, our understanding of fees empowers us to navigate this intricate landscape. Much like the Ferengi's Rule #239, "Never be afraid to mislabel a product," we must not be afraid to unveil the true nature of the fees we encounter.

This section offers practical tips to identify, understand, and mitigate various types of fees. It's a journey where we employ the wisdom of a seasoned Ferengi negotiator—analyzing contracts, comparing options, and advocating for transparency. Through knowledge, we gain the upper hand in a world where fees thrive in the shadows.

The Currency of Literacy

In the Ferengi's universe, education is the cornerstone of success. Our own path to financial success demands a similar cornerstone—financial literacy. As the Ferengi's Rule of Acquisition #74 states, "Knowledge equals profit," our knowledge of fees equals empowerment.

Advocating for financial literacy education is a parallel to the Ferengi's pursuit of knowledge. It's a call to arms to equip ourselves with the tools needed to navigate the fee economy. Just as the Ferengi's commerce flourishes through understanding, our empowerment in the financial world begins with education.

Forging a New Frontier

In the Ferengi's world, profits are garnered through clever deals. In our world, transparency and fairness in fees pave the path toward a new frontier. Just as the Ferengi's Rule of Acquisition #1 asserts, "Once you have their money, never give it back," our society must advocate for fee transparency and fairness to ensure that fees are not extracted under the cloak of confusion.

This section explores grassroots movements and policy initiatives that champion fee transparency and fairness. Much like the Ferengi's pursuit of profit is a shared endeavor, our pursuit of a just fee economy is a shared endeavor—a chorus of voices demanding change, fairness, and accountability.

As we close this chapter, and this book, we're reminded that while the Ferengi's commerce-based culture informs our exploration of fees, our own journey is one of transformation. We are not merely passive participants in a fee economy; we are agents of change, catalysts for reform, and architects of a financial landscape that echoes our values, aspirations, and collective will. The echoes of the Ferengi's pursuit of profit fade into the background, replaced by the resounding call for a financial world where equity, empowerment, and shared prosperity reign supreme.

Chapter 10: The Legal Labyrinth - Navigating Justice for a Price

In a land where commerce reigns supreme, it should come as no surprise that even the halls of justice echo with the clinking of gold-pressed latinum. Welcome to the intersection of legality and profit, where the U.S. criminal justice system dances an intricate tango with the principles of negotiation and plea-bargaining, all under the watchful eyes of the Ferengi Rules of Acquisition.

Rule 14: Anything stolen is pure profit.

In the heart of the American legal maze, defendants often find themselves at a crossroads: to confront the charges head-on or engage in a calculated dance of negotiation. The legal machinery, resembling more of a market bazaar than a temple of justice, values expediency over equity, as defendants bargain away their guilt or innocence like commodities in an auction.

Rule 59: Free advice is seldom cheap.

From flashy attorneys promising the world to well-heeled clients to cutthroat prosecutors seeking high-profile convictions, the American legal landscape is paved with hefty retainers and staggering hourly rates. Justice, it seems, can come with an astronomical price tag, where the depth of one's pockets often determines the quality of defense.

Rule 79: Beware of the Vulcan greed for knowledge.

In the pursuit of knowledge, the U.S. criminal justice system has developed a convoluted playbook of legal maneuvers and precedents. It's a game where every piece of information, every witness testimony, and every shred of evidence is traded like commodities on the stock exchange. Information asymmetry becomes the currency, as those who can manipulate the system best emerge victorious.

Rule 94: Females and finances don't mix.

Gender bias and financial constraints have undeniably intermingled in the realm of justice. Those unable to afford a top-tier attorney often face a troubling paradox: accepting a plea deal, even if unjust, as a pragmatic solution to escape the crushing weight of legal fees and potential prison time. Equity bows to expediency, while the guilty and the innocent alike contemplate the financial gambit of their lives.

Rule 118: When the going gets tough, the tough change the rules.

The Ferengi influence in this arena is stark, with legal twists and turns shaped by the same principles that govern commerce. A defendant's financial prowess often becomes their greatest asset, allowing them to twist the scales of justice in their favor, leveraging their ability to pay for a legal escape hatch while less fortunate individuals languish.

Rule 129: Never ask when you can take.

This chapter unveils a stark reality: the U.S. criminal justice system has morphed into a profit-driven enterprise where morality and ethics can be overshadowed by financial leverage. Plea deals may promise a way out, but they also reveal the uncomfortable truth that one's ability to pay often carries more weight than their moral compass.

Rule 141: Only fools pay retail.

In a system where legal outcomes are often haggled over like prized trinkets, those who can afford to strike a deal often come out ahead. But beneath this veneer lies a troubling conundrum: the scales of justice shouldn't tip based on one's financial muscle but on the intrinsic merit of the case.

As the chapter ends, a sobering realization dawns: the legal labyrinth in the United States has unwittingly embraced the Ferengi way of thinking. What should be a quest for truth, justice, and the betterment of society has too often become a game of financial brinkmanship. It's a system where the accused can buy their way to freedom, where the ethical line between law and commerce blurs, and where the spirit of fairness occasionally bows to the allure of latinum.

But amidst the tangled threads of this dilemma, a glimmer of hope remains. Just as the Ferengi rules can be bent, so can the arc of justice. By challenging the commodification of legal outcomes, advocating for equal access to fair defense, and confronting the very notion that one's fate can be bought, the American people have the power to reshape the legal landscape, steering it away from the realm of commerce and back towards the higher principles it should rightly embrace.

Chapter 11: The Future of Fees

In the vast expanse of the Star Trek universe, where galaxies of possibility unfold, the Ferengi species serve as a mirror reflecting our own commerce-centric culture. As we approach the final chapter of this journey, we stand at a crossroads—a juncture where the future of fees intersects with the echoes of the Ferengi's trading acumen. This chapter is a leap into the abyss of speculation, a reckoning with the inevitable evolution of fees in our "Land of the Fee." Yet, it is also a call to action, a reminder that just as the Ferengi's Rules of Acquisition shape their universe, we have the power to shape our own financial destiny.

The Uncharted Horizon

Imagine a Ferengi speculator contemplating the twists and turns of an uncertain deal—it's a scene that mirrors our own contemplation of the fee landscape in years to come. Just as the Ferengi's Rules of Acquisition evolve with the times, so too does our fee ecosystem adapt to the ever-changing financial landscape. As the Ferengi's Rule #34 states, "War is good for business," we speculate on how the wars of innovation, regulation, and consumer behavior will shape our financial future.

In the Ferengi's pursuit of profit, change is constant; in our pursuit of an equitable fee economy, change should be transformative. This section speculates on the trajectory of fees in years to come—a journey through the warp of technology, the diplomacy of regulation, and the warp core of consumer behavior. The echoes of the Ferengi's commerce-driven ethos meet the uncharted territories of our evolving fee landscape.

The Tech Revolution

In the Ferengi's universe, technology is harnessed for profit. Our own fee landscape undergoes a seismic shift as technology reshapes transactions. Just as the Ferengi's Rule of Acquisition #212 asserts, "Till you can sell it, it ain't worth nothing," technology has the power to enhance, streamline, and even eliminate certain fees.

The role of technology in shaping the fee landscape is akin to the Ferengi's technological ingenuity in trade. As we navigate mobile payments, digital wallets, and blockchain innovations, we see the Ferengi's tenacity for finding profit reflected in our pursuit of more efficient and equitable transactions.

Regulation and Rebellion

In the Ferengi's world, regulations shape the boundaries of commerce. Our world is no different, where regulations can either confine or liberate consumers from fee burdens. As the Ferengi's Rule of Acquisition #68 declares, "Risk is part of the game if you want to sit in that chair," our regulatory game plan shapes the very seat at which we sit.

This section delves into the role of regulation in shaping the fee landscape. It's a battle of interests, where consumers, industry players, and regulators dance the intricate dance of policy-making. Just as the Ferengi's interactions are governed by a strict code, our interactions with the financial system are governed by rules—rules that we have the power to influence and reshape.

The Call to Action

In the Ferengi's universe, their ethos shapes every endeavor. Our own fee future is defined by our ethos—an ethos that demands transparency, fairness, and shared prosperity. Just as the Ferengi's Rule of Acquisition #98 imparts, "Every man has his price," we too have a price—a willingness to demand an equitable and transparent fee economy.

This section encourages readers to take an active role in shaping the fee landscape. It's a call to advocate for transparency, demand fairness, and envision a future where fees are no longer a barrier but a stepping stone to progress. Just as the Ferengi's pursuit of profit is relentless, so too should our pursuit of a financial landscape that mirrors our values and aspirations.

As we conclude this journey through the complexities of financial life, where the Ferengi's commerce-driven culture finds resonance, we're reminded that the future of fees lies not just in our hands, but in our collective determination to chart a course where equity, empowerment, and shared prosperity define our financial future. The echoes of the Ferengi's commerce-driven philosophy meet the call for a fee landscape that transcends profits and resonates with principles—a harmonious cadence where fees serve as instruments of progress rather than barriers to it.

Conclusion: Navigating the Stars of Finance

In the boundless cosmos of Star Trek, where civilizations intersect and diverge, the Ferengi species emerge as a mirror to our commerce-driven culture. As we bid farewell to the journey through "America: Land of the Fee," we stand at the precipice of a transformation—a transformation where the echoes of the Ferengi's Rules of Acquisition merge with our own financial aspirations. This conclusion is not an end, but a launchpad—a launching into a future where the stars of finance align with equity, empowerment, and shared prosperity.

Through the tapestry of chapters, we've voyaged through the intricacies of fees in American society. Just as the Ferengi's pursuit of profit shapes their universe, so too do fees shape ours, interwoven into the fabric of our daily lives. From the hidden charges of convenience to the visible costs of education and healthcare, we've navigated the fee landscape, unveiling parallels between the Ferengi's commerce-driven ethos and our own financial realities.

Yet, the journey is not one of resignation; it's a revelation. We've deciphered the fee code, embarked on the path of financial literacy, and witnessed grassroots movements striving for fee transparency and fairness. We've explored the past, present, and speculated on the future, where technology, regulation, and our own choices define the trajectory of fees.

As we bid adieu, we leave you with these final echoes—a symphony of wisdom drawn from the Ferengi's Rules of Acquisition:

Rule #7: Keep your ears open.

Just as the Ferengi value information, we too must keep our ears open—to the whispers of hidden fees, the melodies of financial opportunities, and the echoes of financial disparities.

Rule #10: Greed is eternal.

Just as the Ferengi's pursuit of profit endures, so too must our pursuit of financial empowerment. But let our greed not be for accumulation alone, but for knowledge, fairness, and progress.

Rule #286: When Morn leaves, it's all over.

As the Ferengi mourn the departure of profit, let us mourn the departure of ignorance. Let the end of ignorance mark the beginning of a journey towards financial understanding.

We've navigated the complexities of the fee landscape, much like the Ferengi navigate the intricacies of commerce. But this journey is not limited by the confines of a book—it extends to the depths of our financial choices, the expanses of our ambitions, and the horizon of our collective vision.

So, as we set forth into the vast unknown, let's do so with purpose, just as the Ferengi approach every deal. Let's equip ourselves with knowledge, just as the Ferengi arm themselves with information. Let's envision a future where the "Land of the Fee" transforms into a land of financial empowerment, fairness, and shared prosperity.

The echoes of the Ferengi's commerce-driven culture fade into the distance, replaced by our own resounding call—a call for a financial landscape where informed decisions pave the way, where fees are transparent and just, and where the stars of finance illuminate a path towards a brighter tomorrow.

Appendix

The Complete Ferengi Rules of Acquisition as featured in the Star Trek series:

1. Once you have their money, you never give it back.
2. The best deal is the one that makes the most profit.
3. Never pay more for an acquisition than you have to.
4. A woman wearing clothes is like a man in the kitchen.
5. If you can't break a contract, bend it.
6. Never let family stand in the way of opportunity.
7. Keep your ears open.
8. Small print leads to large risk.
9. Opportunity plus instinct equals profit.
10. Greed is eternal.
11. Even if it's free, you can always buy it cheaper.
12. Anything worth doing is worth doing for money.
13. Anything worth selling is worth selling twice.
14. Anything stolen is pure profit.
15. Acting stupid is often smart.
16. A deal is a deal, until a better one comes along.
17. A contract is a contract is a contract... but only between Ferengi.
18. A Ferengi without profit is no Ferengi at all.
19. Satisfaction is not guaranteed.
20. He who dives under the table today lives to profit tomorrow.
21. Never place friendship before profit.
22. A wise man can hear profit in the wind.
23. Nothing is more important than your health... except for your money.

24. Latinum lasts longer than lust.
25. You can't make a deal if you're dead.
26. The vast majority of the rich in this galaxy did not inherit their wealth; they stole it.
27. There's nothing more dangerous than an honest businessman.
28. Morality is always defined by those in power.
29. When someone says, "It's not the money," it's the money.
30. Talk is cheap; synthehol costs money.
31. Never make fun of a Ferengi's mother.
32. Be careful what you sell. It may do exactly what the buyer expects.
33. It never hurts to suck up to the boss.
34. War is good for business.
35. Peace is good for business.
36. Only fools pay retail.
37. You can't free a fish from water.
38. Early to bed, early to rise, work like hell, and advertise.
39. Worry is the only real profit.
40. She can touch your lobes but never your latinum.
41. Profit is its own reward.
42. What's mine is mine, and what's yours is mine too.
43. Never trust a beneficiary.
44. Never confuse wisdom with luck.
45. Expand or die.
46. Never say "enough."
47. Never trust a man wearing a better suit than your own.
48. The bigger the smile, the sharper the knife.
49. Old age and greed will always overcome youth and talent.
50. Never bluff a Klingon.
51. Never admit a mistake if there's someone else to blame.
52. Never ask when you can take.
53. Never trust anyone wearing a better suit than your own.
54. Never stab a man in the back when you can stab him in the front.

55. Step on the toes you can't see.
56. Keep your lies consistent.
57. Good customers are as rare as latinum; treasure them.
58. There's no substitute for success.
59. Free advice is seldom cheap.
60. Keep your lies consistent.
61. Every once in a while, declare peace. It confuses the hell out of your enemies.
62. The riskier the road, the greater the profit.
63. Work is the best therapy. So is revenge.
64. Well done is as good as well said.
65. Win or lose, there's always Hupyrian beetle snuff.
66. The secret of staying young is to live honestly, eat slowly, and lie about your age.
67. The secret to diplomacy is letting the other guy have your way.
68. Risk is part of the game if you want to sit in that chair.
69. Never trust a wise man.
70. Trust is the biggest liability of all.
71. There's a customer born every minute.
72. Never let the competition know what you're thinking.
73. If it gets you profit, sell your own grandmother.
74. Knowledge equals profit.
75. Home is where the heart is, but the stars are made of latinum.
76. Every once in a while, declare peace. It confuses the hell out of your enemies.
77. It's better to swallow your pride than to lose your profit.
78. When the going gets tough, the tough change the Rules.
79. Beware the man who doesn't make time for oo-mox.
80. Keep your friends close, but keep your enemies closer.
81. Necessity is the mother of invention. Profit is the father.
82. The flimsier the product, the higher the price.
83. If you break it, you've bought it.
84. A friend is not a friend if he asks for a discount.
85. Never wave to a ship you don't want to board.

86. Never have sex with the boss's sister.
87. If it's free, take it and worry about hidden costs later.
88. There's no better business than peace.
89. Ask not what your profits can do for you; ask what you can do for your profits.
90. New customers are like razor-toothed gree-worms; they can be succulent, but sometimes they bite back.
91. Treat people in your debt like family; exploit them.
92. Give someone a fish, you feed them for a day; sell them a fish, you feed them for a lifetime.
93. Act without delay! The sharp knife cuts quickly.
94. Females and finances don't mix.
95. Expand or die.
96. For every rule, there is an equal and opposite rule. (Also known as the 285th Rule of Acquisition)
97. Enough... is never enough.
98. Every man has his price.
99. Trust is the biggest liability of all.
100. If they take your first offer, you either asked too little or offered too much.
101. The only value of a collectible is what you can get somebody else to pay for it.
102. Nature decays, but latinum lasts forever.
103. Sleep can interfere with opportunity.
104. Faith moves mountains... of inventory.
105. A wife is a luxury... a smart accountant a necessity.
106. There is no honor in poverty.
107. A warranty is valid only if they can find you.
108. Whisper your way to success.
109. Dignity and an empty sack is worth the sack.
110. Wear your creditors like your armor.
111. Treat people in your debt like family; exploit them.
112. Never sleep with the boss's wife unless you pay him first.
113. Always have sex with the boss.

114. Anything stolen is pure profit.
115. When the customer dies, the money stops.
116. There's no such thing as an unfair advantage.
117. Good customers are as rare as latinum; treasure them.
118. When in doubt, lie.
119. Never drink from the same glass as the boss.
120. Both money and friends are better than money alone.
121. If a deal is fairly conducted

, it's a conflict of interest.
122. Beware the Vulcan greed for knowledge.
123. Money is honey.
124. The more they overthink the plumbing, the easier it is to stop up the drain.
125. You can't make a deal if you're dead.
126. Count it.
127. Stay neutral in conflict so that you can sell supplies to both sides.
128. What's in it for me?
129. Never ask when you can take.
130. It's better to beg forgiveness than to ask permission.
131. Never do something you can make someone do for you.
132. Always keep your ears open.
133. Anything free is worth what you pay for it.
134. There is no substitute for success.
135. War is good for business, invest your son.
136. The justification for profit is profit.
137. Buy, sell, or get out of the way.
138. Sleep can interfere with an opportunity.
139. Wives serve, brothers inherit.
140. Money talks, but having a lots of it gets more attention.
141. Only fools pay retail.
142. There's no place like the present.
143. A friend is not a friend if he asks for a discount.

144. There is no substitute for success.
145. The law can be bought; the truth is priceless.
146. When the customer dies, the money stops.
147. Time, like latinum, is a highly limited commodity.
148. Opportunity waits for no one.
149. Sometimes the only thing more dangerous than a question is an answer.
150. Profit is its own reward.
151. You can't free a fish from water.
152. Anything worth selling is worth selling twice.
153. Sell the sizzle, not the steak.
154. A contract without fine print is a fool's contract.
155. When the mouse laughs at the cat, there's a hole nearby.
156. There's no substitute for success.
157. It's better to have your ship blown up in space than be boarded by pirates.
158. The law explicitly favors the rich.
159. Customers are always willing to give a little more for a little less.
160. Never stop till you're done.
161. Never place friendship above the acquisition.
162. Keep your lies consistent.
163. In the end, everything is for sale.
164. Even in the worst of times, someone turns a profit.
165. The higher you bid, the more customers you drive away.
166. Never let a cute girl keep you from making a profit.
167. There's always a catch.
168. Whisper your way to success.
169. Competition and fair play are mutually exclusive.
170. Keep your friends close, but keep your customers closer.
171. Revenge is profit.
172. If you're gonna have to endure, make sure you get paid for it.
173. The early investor reaps the most interest.
174. Keep your women and your politics in separate beds.

175. You can't shake hands with a closed fist.

176. Respect is good; Latinum, better.

177. Know your enemies... but do business with them always.

178. The windfall you were counting on never arrived.

179. Never fight with a Klingon... unless you're sure you can win.

180. Know your enemies... but do business with them always.

181. Not even dishonesty can tarnish the shine of profit.

182. The moment you take your profits is the moment you lose them.

183. Beware the man who doesn't make time for oo-mox.

184. Whenever possible, lie.

185. It's always good business to know about new customers before they walk in your door.

186. A good lie is easier to believe than the truth.

187. The customer is always right... until you have their cash.

188. The more they overthink the plumbing, the easier it is to stop up the drain.

189. The Ferengi are not responsible for the stupidity of other races.

190. Hear all, trust nothing.

191. Assume the worst and you'll never be disappointed.

192. Never cheat a Klingon... unless you're sure you can get away with it.

193. Trouble comes in threes.

194. Anything you can't have isn't worth having.

195. Every man has his price.

196. The best deals are the ones where everyone walks away a little unhappy.

197. The best way to keep a secret is to keep it to yourself. Second best: tell one other person—if you must. There is no third best.

198. Sometimes, what you get free costs entirely too much.

199. Location, location, location.

200. A lie isn't a lie until someone else knows the truth.

201. New customers are like razor-toothed gree-worms. They can be succulent, but sometimes they bite back.

202. The justification for profit is profit.

203. New customers are like razor-toothed gree-worms. They can be succulent, but sometimes they bite back.

204. It takes a smart Ferengi to recognize genius.

205. Don't break the deal that's already working.

206. The selling of good customers as slaves is prohibited.

207. Don't trust anyone who trusts you.

208. Sometimes the only thing as dangerous as a question is an answer.

209. Tell them what they want to hear.

210. Hugs are better than pugs.

211. Employees are the rungs on the ladder to success. Don't hesitate to step on them.

212. Only idiots pay retail.

213. The vast majority of the rich in this galaxy did not inherit their wealth; they stole it.

214. Never begin a business negotiation on an empty stomach.

215. When you're in bed with the boss, sleep with one eye open.

216. Never gamble with a telepath.

217. You can't hit a target you can't see.

218. Always know what you're buying.

219. Possession is eleven-tenths of the law.

220. Man is the only animal that deals.

221. There's a difference between moving on and moving forward.

222. The rule of acquisition number 222, only in the DS9 season 7, episode 12: "The Emperor's New Cloak".

223. Beware the man who doesn't make time for oo-mox.

224. Never confuse wisdom with luck.

225. You're never too old for anything if you can still do it.

226. Don't kill a customer unless you're sure you'll get paid.

227. You can get away with anything as long as you don't do it in public.

228. Nothing is more important than your health... except for your money.
229. Latinum isn't the only thing that shines.
230. Sometimes, what you get free costs entirely too much.
231. Sometimes, the only thing more dangerous than a question is an

answer.
232. The customer is always right, the seller, even more so.
233. Everything is for sale, including friendship.
234. Your top hat is worth more than your top dollar.
235. The customer may always be right, but that doesn't mean you have to do business with them.
236. You can't buy fate.
237. It never hurts to suck up to the boss.
238. Everything is worth something to somebody.
239. Never be afraid to mislabel a product.
240. Time, like Latinum, is a highly limited commodity.
241. You gotta have patience, patience leads to profit.
242. More is good... all is better.
243. Never offer a confession when a bribe will do.
244. The right to rich customers is the right to all customers.
245. If you're willing to sell gossip, be ready to buy it.
246. Anyone worth shooting is worth shooting twice.
247. A press conference is a good way to ruin a good deal.
248. The definition of insanity is trying the same failed schemes over and over and expecting different results.
249. When it's good for business, tell the truth.
250. The future is always changing.
251. She can touch your lobes, but never your latinum.
252. Never gamble with an empath.
253. Profit has limits; losses have none.
254. Often, a hard heart is no good for profit.
255. A wife is a luxury... a smart accountant, a necessity.

256. Money can't buy happiness, but you can sure have a blast renting it.

257. The greater the smile, the sharper the knife.

258. Choose your enemies wisely, and you'll never have to kill them.

259. Latinum lasts longer than lust.

260. Never confuse wisdom with luck.

261. A wealthy man can afford anything except a conscience.

262. If you manipulate the data enough, it'll confess to anything.

263. Never let doubt interfere with your lust for Latinum.

264. You can't always get what you want, unless you're dealing with the Dopterians.

265. Never trust a beneficiary.

266. When in doubt, lie.

267. There are three things that are real: Latinum and women and ships.

268. If you deceive your clients, you risk your freedom.

269. Your customers know more about your business than you do.

270. In business deals, a disruptor can be almost as important as a calculator.

271. Any change is good... except the change in your pocket.

272. The definition of insanity is trying the same failed schemes over and over again expecting different results.

273. For every 10,000 darseks you earn, I get 5 bars of gold-pressed latinum.

274. Laws are always subject to interpretation; keep the crybabies hungry.

275. There's nothing wrong with charity... as long as it winds up in your pocket.

276. Every man has his price.

277. Anything worth selling is worth selling twice.

278. Anything worth selling is worth selling twice.

279. Always inspect the merchandise before making a deal.

280. Fear makes a good business partner.

281. By listening to your customers, you earn money.
282. The more you give your customer, the more they give you.
283. You can't erase a debt by talking.
284. Deep down, everyone's a Ferengi.
285. No good deed ever goes unpunished.
286. When Morn leaves, it's all over.
287. no canon text, only name mentioned in DS9 Season 7 episode 12 "The Emperor's New Cloak"
288. no canon text, only name mentioned in DS9 Season 7 episode 12 "The Emperor's New Cloak"
289. Never bet on a race you haven't fixed.
290. Friendship is temporary, profit is forever.
291. Never buy what can be stolen.
292. When the price is high enough, you can sell your own mother.
293. The more you spend on shipping, the smaller the profits.
294. Latinum can't buy happiness, but you can sure have a blast renting it.
295. Make up the rules as you go along.
296. The justification for profit is profit.
297. There's no honor in poverty.
298. There is no honor in poverty.
299. After you've exploited someone, it never hurts to thank them. That way, it's easier to exploit them next time.
300. After you've exploited someone, it never hurts to thank them. That way, it's easier to exploit them next time.
301. If it's free, take it and worry about hidden costs later.
302. The more they tell you, the more you want to know.
303. When two Ferengi are in business, it's the first Ferengi's business. When three Ferengi are in business, it's the second Ferengi's business.
304. She can touch your lobes, but never your latinum.
305. In a dispute, both sides feel pain.
306. The faster the ship, the smaller the profit.

307. Tell the truth or someone will tell it for you.

308. Trust is the biggest liability of all.

309. One can never underestimate the power of the pout.

310. The key to a woman's heart is through her jeweler.

311. Never turn your back on a Breen.

312. Never trust a creature wearing a suit.

313. Plan for tomorrow, but don't be surprised if you don't have one.

314. Never cheat a wealthy man unless you're sure you can get away with it.

315. Always give your customers a present when you're closing a deal.

316. There's always a way out.

317. Profit is a woman's best friend.

318. If you don't have the latinum, you can't buy the goods.

319. Never apologize when you can fake sincerity.

320. Competition and fair play are mutually exclusive.

321. no canon text, only name mentioned in DS9 Season 7 episode 12 "The Emperor's New Cloak"

322. It's never wise to underestimate the competition.

323. no canon text, only name mentioned in DS9 Season 7 episode 12 "The Emperor's New Cloak"

324. Never gamble with a telepath.

325. Anything worth fighting for is worth hiding from.

326. It's better to have your ship blown up in space than to be boarded by pirates.

327. Never confuse wisdom with luck.

328. If you want to keep a secret, keep it. Don't tell anyone.

329. The more you want, the less you get.

330. Open mouths mean open minds.

331. Never take anyone's advice.

332. Never give away for free what can be sold.

333. You can't make a deal if you're dead.

334. The fire you can walk through, the fire that burns you.

335. Listen to secrets, but never repeat them.

336. Never trust a hoo-mahn.

337. Profit has limits; losses have none.

338. If you can't buy it, make it yourself.

339. No good deed ever goes unpunished.

340. War is a dangerous business; you never know who's watching you.

341. If it's new, it's for sale; if it's old, it's for sale;

if it's blue, sell it.

342. The only value of a collectible is what you can get somebody else to pay for it.

343. Don't trust a man wearing a better suit than your own.

344. Take all that you can get, and give nothing back.

345. The only thing more dangerous than a Ferengi with a good business deal, is a Ferengi with a good wormhole.

346. The odds are always in the house's favor.

347. With good grammar, you can convince anyone of anything.

348. Don't trust anyone who trusts you.

349. Diamond necklace or handcuffs, the choice is yours.

350. Money equals power. Blink of an Eye (VOY episode)

How Ferengi Rules of Acquisition Connect With Business In America today:

Rule 1: Once you have their money, never give it back.
   This rule reflects the profit-oriented nature of business in America. Companies often focus on maximizing revenue and retaining customer payments, sometimes at the expense of customer satisfaction.

Rule 3: Never spend more for an acquisition than you have to.

In the American business landscape, companies often engage in cost-cutting measures to ensure profitability. Negotiating favorable deals and seeking cost-efficient solutions are common practices. In America, cost-effectiveness is a fundamental principle in business. Companies aim to minimize expenses and negotiate better deals to maximize their profits.

Rule 6: Never allow family to stand in the way of opportunity.
In American business, the pursuit of opportunities often takes precedence over personal relationships. Family ties might sometimes be secondary when business prospects arise, especially in competitive industries.

Rule 7: Keep your ears open.
   Staying informed and attentive to market trends, customer feedback, and industry changes is crucial for businesses to remain competitive and make informed decisions.

Rule 8: Small print leads to large risk.
   Companies often bury important terms and conditions in fine print, contracts, and agreements, taking advantage of customers' lack of attention to detail. This is commonly seen in terms of service agreements, where users unknowingly agree to certain conditions that may not be in their favor.

Rule 10: Greed is eternal.
   The pursuit of profits and market dominance remains a driving force in American capitalism, leading companies to continuously strive for expansion and financial success.

Rule 13: Anything worth doing is worth doing for money.
   This rule resonates with the monetization of hobbies, skills, and creative pursuits. Many Americans turn their passions into

profitable ventures through platforms like e-commerce, content creation, and freelancing.

Rule 14: Anything stolen is pure profit.
    This rule can reflect practices like intellectual property theft, patent infringement, and unauthorized use of copyrighted material, which can lead to financial gains for some American businesses.

Rule 16: A deal is a deal, until a better one comes along.
    Business deals in America often involve negotiation and adaptation to changing circumstances, as companies aim to secure the best possible terms for themselves.

Rule 18: A Ferengi without profit is no Ferengi at all.
    The emphasis on profitability aligns with the core principle of American capitalism, where businesses strive to generate revenue and maintain sustainable growth.

Rule 21: Never place friendship above the acquisition.
    While relationships and networking are essential in American business, companies often prioritize opportunities for financial gain over personal connections.

Rule 22: A wise man can hear profit in the wind.
    - Successful entrepreneurs in the U.S. have a knack for identifying profitable opportunities and adapting to changing market conditions to stay ahead.

Rule 23: Nothing is more important than your health... except for your money.
    This rule highlights the focus on financial success in American culture, sometimes leading to work-related stress and prioritizing wealth over personal well-being.

Rule 31: Never make fun of a Ferengi's mother.

In American business, respecting cultural sensitivities and avoiding offensive content is essential for maintaining positive public relations and avoiding backlash.

Rule 33: It never hurts to suck up to the boss.

Brown-nosing or trying to impress higher-ups is a common strategy in American workplaces to gain favor, promotions, and better opportunities.

Rule 34: War is good for business, invest your son.

The defense industry in America is a significant contributor to the economy, and military conflicts can impact various sectors, highlighting the financial implications of warfare.

Rule 35: Peace is good for business.

Similarly, peace and stability create a conducive environment for economic growth in America, allowing businesses to flourish without disruptions.

Rule 41: Profit is its own reward.

In the pursuit of profit, American businesses prioritize financial success and often measure their achievements based on revenue and returns.

Rule 47: Never trust a man wearing a better suit than your own.

This rule reflects the competitive nature of American business, where appearances and attire can influence perceptions and business interactions.

Rule 48: The bigger the smile, the sharper the knife.

In negotiations and sales, outward friendliness and charm may hide underlying business motives and strategies, reflecting the complexity of American business relationships.

Rule 57: Good customers are as rare as latinum. Treasure them.

Building and retaining a loyal customer base is a cornerstone of American business. Companies often invest in customer loyalty programs to maintain valuable long-term relationships.

Rule 58: There is no profit in peace.

The defense industry in America thrives during times of conflict or uncertainty, and military interventions have often been tied to economic gains, reflecting the sentiment of this rule.

Rule 59: Free advice is seldom cheap.

Despite the seemingly altruistic nature of free advice, individuals and businesses in America often question the motives behind such offers, recognizing potential hidden costs or agendas.

Rule 68: Risk is our business.

American business culture encourages calculated risk-taking as a means to innovate, grow, and seize opportunities, acknowledging that risk and reward go hand in hand.

Rule 74: Knowledge equals profit.

The value of data and information has grown immensely in America's tech-driven economy. Companies that possess valuable insights often turn them into profits by offering data-driven products and services.

Rule 75: Home is where the heart is, but the stars are made of latinum.

- Businesses in America often expand their operations beyond domestic borders to tap into international markets and revenue streams.

Rule 76: Every once in a while, declare peace. It confuses the hell out of your enemies.

Temporarily shifting business strategies or entering into peaceful collaborations can disrupt competitors' expectations and provide new avenues for success in American business.

Rule 87: Learn the customer's weaknesses, so that you can better take advantage of them.

- Marketing strategies in the U.S. often involve targeting consumer preferences and vulnerabilities to drive sales and brand loyalty.

Rule 94: Females and finances don't mix.

This rule highlights gender disparities that persist in American workplaces, emphasizing the need for equality and fairness in business environments.

Rule 98: Every man has his price.

This rule resonates with lobbying practices in America, where individuals or corporations might seek influence or policy changes by contributing to political campaigns or interest groups.

Rule 102: Nature decays, but Latinum lasts forever.

While not directly about environmental concerns, this rule reminds us that the focus on profit can sometimes overshadow considerations for sustainable and ethical practices.

Rule 103: Sleep can interfere with an opportunity.

- In the fast-paced world of American business, being responsive and seizing opportunities quickly can lead to success, sometimes at the cost of personal rest

Rule 109: Dignity and an empty sack is worth the sack.

In a consumer-driven society, the pursuit of material possessions and status often takes precedence over personal values. People may compromise their principles for the sake of perceived success or wealth.

Rule 110: Employ family; they appreciate you more.
Family-run businesses and close-knit corporate cultures are common in America, where personal connections can contribute to loyalty and commitment among employees.

Rule 111: Treat people in your debt like family; exploit them.
This rule can be seen in how businesses use customer loyalty programs, credit cards, and financial products to keep individuals engaged and spending.

Rule 125: You can't make a deal if you're dead.
The rule underscores the importance of personal well-being and decision-making in American business, emphasizing that individuals need to be alive and well to engage in transactions and negotiations.

Rule 139: Wives serve, brothers inherit.
Although outdated in today's society, this rule points to historical gender biases in inheritance and family-owned businesses. It highlights the historical inequality faced by women in business and property rights.

Rule 144: There's nothing wrong with charity... as long as it winds up in your pocket.
This rule highlights the idea that even philanthropy in America can have strategic motivations, such as enhancing a company's reputation or creating positive public relations.

Rule 151: Never trust a beneficiary.

This rule highlights the skepticism that can arise in business situations, as American companies often question the intentions of partners, clients, and collaborators.

Rule 162: Even in the worst of times, someone turns a profit.
Economic downturns or crises often see certain industries profiting by providing solutions or services that capitalize on the situation, illustrating the truth of this rule.

Rule 168: Whisper your way to success.
- Networking, negotiations, and confidential business dealings often involve sharing information discreetly to gain advantages.

Rule 190: Hear all, trust nothing.
In the age of data breaches and cybersecurity concerns, American businesses must be vigilant and cautious about sharing sensitive information to protect themselves and their clients.

Rule 202: The justification for profit is profit.
This rule captures the essence of capitalism in America, where businesses prioritize profitability as the ultimate measure of success and sustainability.

Rule 211: Employees are the rungs on the ladder to success. Don't hesitate to step on them.
While not a literal interpretation, this rule reflects certain business cultures where employees are seen as expendable and are sometimes treated as such to maximize profits.

Rule 214: Never begin a business negotiation on an empty stomach.
Business meals and networking events in America provide opportunities to build relationships and conduct negotiations in a

more relaxed setting, emphasizing the importance of interpersonal interactions.

Rule 223: Beware the man who doesn't make time for oo-mox.
 This playful rule highlights the importance of relationships and networking in American business, as social interactions and networking events often lead to professional opportunities.

Rule 229: Latinum isn't the only thing that shines.
 In America's celebrity-driven culture, personal branding and public image can play a significant role in business success, reflecting the idea that not everything valuable is tangible.

 Rule 239: Never be afraid to mislabel a product.
 This rule connects to deceptive marketing practices that may exaggerate the benefits or features of a product to attract customers, even if the claims are not entirely accurate.

Rule 242: More is good... all is better.
 This rule reflects the American mindset of growth and expansion. Businesses often seek to maximize their operations, markets, and offerings to achieve greater success.

Rule 255: A wife is a luxury... a smart accountant, a necessity.
 This rule's implication can be extended to recognizing the importance of financial management and planning, with businesses often relying on accountants for fiscal responsibility.

Rule 263: Never let doubt interfere with your lust for Latinum.
 Doubt and hesitation can hinder business opportunities. In the pursuit of profits, some businesses prioritize taking risks and seizing opportunities even when uncertainty exists.

Rule 268: Trust is the biggest liability of all.

In a litigious society, businesses often emphasize detailed contracts and legal protections, reflecting the idea that trust can lead to vulnerabilities in certain situations.

Rule 286: When Morn leaves, it's all over.
This humorous rule could symbolize the importance of customer loyalty. When a valued customer or client leaves, it could signify potential trouble for a business, emphasizing the significance of retaining customers.

These connections demonstrate how the Ferengi Rules of Acquisition can often find parallels in the strategies and practices of American businesses, highlighting the complex interplay between profit motives, relationships, and market dynamics.